Green Smoothies: The Weight Loss & Detox Secret

By Jonathan Vine

Green Smoothies:
The Weight Loss & Detox Secret

50 Recipes for a Healthy Diet

by

Jonathan Vine

Copyright Information

DISCLAIMER

Table of Contents

Introduction

Forget what you think you know about fast food. Our lives are lived faster. We have to accommodate our busy schedules, so we opt for drive-through foods, processed foods, and unnatural foods to feed our bodies. We make excuses to ourselves that we do not have the time, the money, or the energy needed to eat healthier and continue to press forward in our routines that have gotten hold of us, and our health.

Choosing to eat healthier is a lifestyle choice. It involves a commitment to life better lived, beginning with the conscious decision to fuel the human body with foods that it was created to eat. Our bodies were not meant to digest massive amounts of meat, sugar, and processed foods. To run efficiently, our bodies cannot be hampered with too much white flour or chemically enhanced foods. Our bodies were hardwired to taste, enjoy, and digest plants foods.

Let me introduce to you the newest fast food: the green smoothie. This mixture of sun ripened fruits and earth harvested vegetables can be made in seconds. You can say "Goodbye," to the regret that normally comes along with eating fast food.

Green smoothies are nutritious—providing your body with vitamins, minerals, and anti-oxidants. Packed with nutrients used to fight diseases such as diabetes, cancer, and heart disease, you will begin to wonder why you have gone so long without enjoying green smoothies.

And for those who are thinking, "I just don't like vegetables. I don't care how good they are for me," there is a wide array of ingredients to choose from. When these potentially bitter tasting vegetables are blended with other vegetables and fruits, the flavors mix together to create an entirely new one that is enjoyable. You can mix them to your own liking.

We even include a list of tips that we have found helpful since we have made the commitment to ourselves to live a healthier, fuller life by drinking green smoothies.

CHAPTER 1 - What is a Green Smoothie?

A green smoothie is a delicious blend of fruits, vegetables, nuts, herbs, and spices—all of the foods that the body needs to run most efficiently.

Some of ingredients that can be used in a green smoothie are as followed:

Apples - source of fiber, aids in digestion, regulates blood sugar.

Avocado - anti-inflammatory, helps lower heart disease

Berries – antioxidants.

Broccoli - lowers cholesterol, excellent source of vitamins A and D.

Cabbage - lowers cholesterol, cancer fighting food.

Carrots - beta-carotene, produces vitamin A .

Cucumber - loaded with antioxidants, reduces risk of

cancer and cardiovascular disease.

Herbs - protect against cancer, diabetes, heart disease

Kale - cancer protection, lowers cholesterol, antioxidants, fiber.

Nuts and seeds - prevent against heart disease.

Pears - loaded with antioxidants, cancer fighting food.

Plant based milk (soy, almond, coconut) - protein,

calcium, vitamins A, B, E, iron, magnesium.

Spinach - iron, antioxidants, calcium, potassium, cancer protection, lowers cholesterol.

Sweetener (maple syrup, honey, agave syrup) - antioxidants.

Yogurt - probiotics, vitamins, protein.

Zucchini - loaded with antioxidants.

This is not an exhaustive list; there are so many more options available!

So now that you know what some of the ingredients are that go into green smoothies, you might be wondering what the benefits are in eating them blended as opposed to whole or cooked. Continue onto chapter 2 to find out why!

CHAPTER 2 – What's So Good About Green Smoothies?

The fundamental idea behind a green smoothie is to provide the maximum amount of nutrition in one drink. Forget about fast food as you have come to know it. This quick and convenient mixture of healthy fruits and vegetables gives you the majority of your daily needs without having to take extra supplements to meet your daily nutritional requirements.

We get the most nutritional value out of fruits and vegetables when they are consumed in their raw state. Cooking vegetables often reduces the overall nutritional value while blending them still retains it. But for those of you who might be wondering why not just eat the fruits and vegetables raw—do eat them raw! But if you want the convenience of maximum nutrition at one go with the delicious flavor—blend! According to a survey, blended foods are digested and absorbed quicker into the body than regular chewing—as much as 90% more!

You don't like some of the vegetables? Blend the veggies that you would otherwise dismiss for being less than tasty. Even kids love them!

Did you know that some studies conducted in the USA show that one third of children do not consume two cups of fruit or vegetables daily? Green smoothies are the best way to get all of what you need into the bodies that you love.

For those who are saying "I eat a salad daily; I eat healthy." Yes, salads are better than pizza and cheeseburgers; however, they still contain dressings that are loaded with fat and sugar. A green smoothie does not have anything processed—it is all natural.

Not only are they convenient and delicious, drinking green smoothies on a consistent basis offers so many nutritional benefits and impacts long term health.

CHAPTER 3 – Nutritional Value

After having read the list of potential ingredients that go into green smoothies, there is no denying that green smoothies are absolutely nutritious!

Dark leafy greens offer antioxidants, vitamins, and minerals. They contain alkaline which helps in neutralizing the acids in our blood. If blended with fruits heavy in vitamin C, some of the minerals, like iron, becomes better absorbed into the body.

Fruits and vegetables provide fiber—which aids in overall digestive health. They provide carbohydrates—the means to your daily energy. Many vegetables, like broccoli, have protein—the food for muscle growth. Green smoothies have potassium, manganese, niacin, chlorophyll—all of the elements that are conducive to overall health and maximum energy. They have what we, as humans, are meant to digest.

So how does this impact overall health?

CHAPTER 4 - Health Benefits of Green Smoothies

So what happens when you commit to a healthy lifestyle choice and begin to drink green smoothies on a regular basis? What's the pay off?

Green smoothies help flush unwanted toxins from your body; they aid in overall digestive health. A healthy digestive track is less prone to cancer in the long run.

Drinking green smoothies on a regular basis stabilizes blood sugar and increases immunity to sickness—both acute and long term. The antioxidants prevent diseases. When a body has all of its nutritional needs met, it will prevent illnesses. You will heal faster too.

Not only will the body be healthier, but the mind will become more clear and receptive. Green smoothies offer all of the nutrients needed for maximum health. You will have more energy to do the things you love to do. Your mental clarity and overall health will improve when you are giving the body what it needs, which will reduce anxiety and stress.

Because of the toxin reducing qualities of green smoothies, your skin will become clearer! If you suffer from acne, are you aware that most acne treatments are only surface level fixes? If you habitually drink green smoothies, then the body receives the nutrients it needs to ward off craving for sweet foods that cause acne. Chlorophyll, a blood purifier present in the green leafy vegetables, flushes the toxins out of the body—which leads to a fresh complexion. It also improves the metabolism rate of healing cells. Vitamin A is a potent nutrient that helps in rebuilding connective tissue. Vitamin K improves skin tone and reduces marks. Sulfur detoxifies and maintains the level of PH in body.

If you are thinking that you could take other forms of vitamins or supplements to get the same result—you just cannot. Our bodies are made to absorb and process the energy from a plant based diet—not a synthetic one.

Not only do green smoothies give you the health you need to do the things you love, they will help you lose weight.

CHAPTER 5 - Green Smoothies- The Healthiest Weight Loss Program

There is a rising consciousness of health in cultures all over the world. We are eating healthier, exercising more, and living longer.

How many of you have tried to diet and have failed because you starve yourself of the foods your body naturally needs and then cut loose after you have restricted yourself for so long and jumped back into eating whatever you wanted? That has happened to many of us and it will continue to happen until you decide to make the conscious decision to commit yourself to healthier eating choices. The choice has never been easier or more right than now.

If you were to replace your breakfast and lunch with a green smoothie and eat a well balanced dinner of whole grains, fruits, vegetables, and protein (complete proteins such as eggs, beans and rice, beans and corn, quinoa), then you would flush the toxins out of your body and stabilize your digestive regularity which WILL lead to weight loss.

If you replaced all of the junk food you normally eat with all natural foods like fresh mangoes or crunchy celery, then you will lose weight. It is not magic; it is science. If your body is fueled with the right foods, it will do more for you. Your cravings for junk food will eventually subside because you are giving your body what it needs. And all of this costs less than supplements, gym memberships, or dieticians.

If you think you are ready to give this a shot, keep reading to find out what types of smoothies you will enjoy.

CHAPTER 6 - Types of Green Smoothies

Depending on what your goals are for beginning your new commitment to the healthier you, there are some options available to all!

For those of you who are concerned with weight loss, we recommend the Low Fat Green Smoothie. The ingredients in this smoothie are mostly veggies, some fruit, and water. Fruit has natural sugars in them and if eaten in excess, will not aid in the reduction of weight.

If you are less worried about the weight as you are the taste or other health benefits, then try the Creamy Green Smoothie. For this smoothie, you add about half veggies, half fruit, and any milk or cream based product. You can try yogurt—which is high in protein or low fat milk if you like a thinner consistency.

And for those of you who love to eat seasonal foods, there is a green smoothie comprised of fruits and vegetables that are in season: the Seasonal Green Smoothie. Use zucchini in the summer for the lighter, crisp flavor or butternut squash in the fall for that warmer, earthy taste. Toss in an apple with the squash for a sweet, yet savory blend of nature's wholesome goodness.

Okay, so you are convinced that green smoothies are the way to go. You know what they are, why they are so good for you, and what types there are for you to make. Keep reading for some helpful tips!

CHAPTER 7 – Tasty Tips

*Drink two smoothies a day for maximum nutrition!

*Green smoothies are way healthier than just fruit smoothies—load up on the veggies!

*Start with adding more fruits in the beginning in case you don't like all of the veggies. Slowly reduce the amount of fruit over time.

*Add a lemon to make it tangier.

 *Add some ginger, cinnamon, or vanilla.

*Replacing water with milk or cream will make it smoother—but it will add more fat to the green smoothie.

*Use ice cubes to chill or thicken.

*Add flax seeds—a rich source of fiber.

*Invest in a quality blender that can handle ice and nuts.

*Put liquid in first so the blades will move freely.

*For smoother drinks, remove stems from kale, chard, other greens, and herbs.

*Only use small amount of sweetener!

*Try to incorporate healthy fats like avocado and coconut oil.

* Add a pinch of salt for the savory smoothies.

*Try superfoods like goji berries, aloe vera, spirulina, and acai.

*Try to be consistent with the time of day that you consume your green smoothie to get your body regular. Prepare one first thing in the morning, or have one within twenty minutes after your morning workout. Have another at lunch time.

CHAPTER 8 – Conclusion

We often picture our future selves down some distant road without realizing that the only way to reach that future is by making choices now that will lead us there. If you have tried dieting and have failed—it is no wonder—our human bodies are meant to eat delicious foods. We love bright, colorful foods that are appealing to the eye. We have a natural sweet tooth because of tasting the fruits of the land's bounty. Drinking green smoothies gives us the best foods our bodies need.

They are a healthy way to get your entire daily intake of vegetables and fruit. Green smoothies are a rich source of vitamins, minerals, fiber, and protein. They prevent chronic illnesses like cancer, diabetes, and heart disease because they are rich in antioxidants, they detoxify the body, and will lead to weight reduction.

Not only are they good for you, but they tasty and the whole family will enjoy them. What more can you give your children than the fuel to energize them? If you introduce healthy life choices to them now, they will not have to convince themselves down some future road to make a commitment because you have already showed them how to do it.

The present choice is yours.

Recipes

Apple and Spinach Smoothie

This smoothie is a classic! The ingredients are common, but they're not to be ignored given the fact that they both are a bomb of fibers and antioxidants. The final smoothie is great for digestion, but also for your immune system. Just a touch of ginger makes this smoothie not only healthier, but also more fragrant.

Servings: 4

Ingredients:

- 2 cups baby spinach
- 2 green apples, cored and sliced
- 1 teaspoon grated ginger
- 1 teaspoon lemon juice
- 2 tablespoons honey
- 1 cup yogurt
- ½ cup crushed ice

Directions:

Combine all the ingredients in a blender and pulse until smooth.

Pour the drink in glasses of your choice and serve it as fresh as possible.

Nutritional information per serving

Calories: 128

Fat: 0.8g

Protein: 3.9g

Carbohydrates: 26.4g

Watercress Chocolate Smoothie

Watercress is definitely not a common ingredient for drinks, but think about it like a type of lettuce. It's slightly bitter, but it has plenty of folate, potassium and vitamin C, as well as iron and iodine. It has been proven to help improve anemia and glucose level in the blood so it is recommended for diabetics as long as they replace the honey with an artificial sweetener.

Servings: 4

Ingredients:

- 1 cup watercress
- 2 cups almond milk
- 1 tablespoons raw cocoa powder
- ½ ripe banana
- 1 tablespoon chia seeds
- 6ice cubes

Directions:

Mix all the ingredients in your blender and pulse until smooth.

Pour the smoothie in glasses of your choice and serve it as fresh as possible as it tends to lose nutrients in time.

Nutritional information per serving

Calories: 333

Fat: 31.2g

Protein: 5g

Carbohydrates: 13.4g

Arugula and Raspberry Smoothie

Arugula, just like any other green leaf vegetable, is loaded with nutrients, but it also has a low caloric content and that makes it perfect for weight loss. The raspberry are not only healthy, but most of all fragrant and boost the taste of the drink. Feel free to replace the arugula with spinach or kale if you want.

Servings: 4

Ingredients:

- 1 cup fresh arugula
- 1 cup fresh or frozen raspberries
- 1 cup fresh orange juice
- 4 ice cubes
- 1 cup plain yogurt
- 2 tablespoons agave syrup
- 1 tablespoon flax seeds

Directions:

Combine all the ingredients in your blender. Pulse until smooth then pour the smoothie in glasses of your choice and serve it as fresh as possible.

Nutritional information per serving

Calories: 178

Fat: 1.6g

Protein: 4.8g

Carbohydrates: 36.2g

Almond and Strawberry Smoothie

This smoothie truly tastes like dessert and you will love its richness and beautiful pink color. Replace the strawberries with blueberries, raspberries or even cherries and you will get a whole new drink with a different taste and a high nutritional profile.

Servings: 4

Ingredients:

- ¼ cup blanched almonds
- 1 cup almond milk
- 1 cup fresh spinach
- 1 cup fresh strawberries

- 1 tablespoon honey
- ½ ripe banana
- 1 teaspoon lemon juice
- 4 ice cubes

Directions:

Combine all the ingredients in your blender and pulse until smooth.

Pour the smoothie in glasses of your choice and serve it immediately as it tends to lose nutrients in time.

Nutritional information per serving

Calories: 215

Fat: 17.4g

Protein: 3.2g

Carbohydrates: 15.3g

Kale, Tomato and Cucumber Smoothie

This drink is rather savory, but don't avoid it because of that! You will be surprised to discover a chilled and delicious drink that has the consistency and taste of a soup. For that reason, it is best enjoyed in the afternoon of evening.

Servings: 4

Ingredients:

- 2 ripe tomatoes, peeled and seeded
- 1 cucumber, peeled
- ¼ celery stalk
- 6 kale leaves
- 1 cup water
- ½ cup plain yogurt
- 1 tablespoon chia seeds
- 6 ice cubes

Directions:

Combine all the ingredients in your blender and pulse until smooth.

Pour the drink in glasses of your choice and serve it as fresh as possible in order to preserve the nutrients.

Nutritional information per serving

Calories: 133

Fat: 3g

Protein: 7.3g

Carbohydrates: 20.5g

Minty Avocado Smoothie

How can you not love a rich and yet refreshing smoothie?! The avocado is responsible for the richness of this drink, but then mint is added to mellow it down and turn it into a great drink for summer.

Servings: 4

Ingredients:

- ½ ripe avocado, peeled
- 2 cups almond milk
- 2 mint leaves
- 2 tablespoons agave syrup
- ½ cup plain yogurt
- ½ cup crushed ice

Directions:

Mix all the ingredients in a blender and pulse until smooth.

Pour the drink in glasses and serve it right away as it tends to change color in time.

Nutritional information per serving

Calories: 389

Fat: 35g

Protein: 5.4g

Carbohydrates: 21.2g

All-Green Smoothie

You can't have a green smoothie book without this all-green smoothie recipe, can you?! This drink is a real bomb of nutrients, being packed with antioxidants, iron, potassium, calcium and plenty of fibers. The banana is there just to thicken it up and boost the taste, but skip adding it if you're looking for weight loss.

Servings: 4

Ingredients:

- 6 kale leaves
- 1 cup fresh spinach
- 1 Swiss chard leaf
- 1 green apple, cored and sliced
- ½ celery stalk
- 1 ripe banana
- 1 cup almond milk
- ½ cup crushed ice
- 2 tablespoons honey
- 1 teaspoon lemon juice
- ½ teaspoon lemon zest

Directions:

Combine all the ingredients in your blender and process until smooth.

Pour the drink in glasses of your choice and serve it immediately as it tends to lose color and nutrients in time.

Nutritional information per serving

Calories: 278

Fat: 15.8g

Protein: 4.4g

Carbohydrates: 34.2g

Swiss Chard and Cantaloupe Smoothie

Both Swiss chard and cantaloupe are summer fruits and veggies but you would never expect them to taste so well into the same smoothie recipe. It's an amazing and cooling recipe that will boost your energy level while helping your stomach stay healthy.

Servings: 4

Ingredients:

- 1 ½ cups cantaloupe cubes
- 4 Swiss chard leaves
- 1 teaspoon lemon juice
- 1 tablespoon honey
- 2 mint leaves
- ½ cup plain yogurt
- ½ cup crushed ice

Directions:

Combine all the ingredients in your blender and pulse until well mixed and smooth.

Pour the drink in glasses and serve it immediately as it tends to lose nutrients in time.

Nutritional information per serving

Calories: 109

Fat: 2.2g

Protein: 4.2g

Carbohydrates: 15.6g

Watermelon and Spinach Smoothie

Watermelon is watery and great to restore your water level. That makes it perfect for summer. However, don't be fooled by its water content because watermelon has a good amount of natural sugar too. So if you're looking for weight loss, it might not be your best choice.

Servings: 4

Ingredients:

- 2 cups fresh spinach
- 1 cup seedless watermelon cubes
- ¼ cup coconut cream
- 1 cup coconut water
- 1 tablespoon lemon juice
- 2 mint leaves
- 4 ice cubes

Directions:

Combine all the ingredients in a blender and pulse until smooth.

Pour the drink in glasses and serve the smoothie as fresh as possible.

<u>Nutritional information per serving</u>

Calories: 64

Fat: 3.8g

Protein: 1.5g

Carbohydrates: 7g

Kale Blueberry Smoothie

Kale can be rather tough to blend, but here is a tip to obtain a smooth drink: remove the stems from each kale leaf. The nutrients remain the same, but the drink will be smoother and creamier.

Servings: 4

Ingredients:

- 1 cup fresh or frozen blueberries
- 6 kale leaves, stems removed
- 1 cup buttermilk
- 2 tablespoons honey
- ½ cup crushed ice

Directions:

Combine all the ingredients in a blender and pulse until smooth.

Pour the drink in glasses and serve it as fresh and chilled.

Nutritional information per serving

Calories: 127

Fat: 0.7g

Protein: 5.3g

Carbohydrates: 27.4g

Celery and Apple Smoothie

Celery is a great source of fibers and vitamin C, as well as other antioxidants, but it has a rather intense taste on its own. That is when the apples step in, mellowing down the taste of celery and creating a delicious smoothie. However, the apple can be replaced with any other fruit if you like.

Servings: 4

Ingredients:

- 1 celery stalk, chopped
- 2 kale leaves
- 2 green apples, cored and sliced
- 1 pinch cinnamon powder
- 2 tablespoons raw honey
- 1 lime, juiced and zested
- 1 cup plain yogurt
- 4 ice cubes

Directions:

Mix all the ingredients in your blender.

Pulse until smooth then pour the drink in glasses of your choice and serve.

Nutritional information per serving

Calories: 145

Fat: 1g

Protein: 4.7g

Carbohydrates: 30.9g

Beet and Broccoli Smoothie

I know this combination sounds weird and far from tasty, but it is a savory smoothie and it does its job well: restores your energy level and loads your system with vitamin A, C, potassium, iron and calcium.

Servings: 4

Ingredients:

- 1 large raw beet, juiced
- 1 cup broccoli florets
- 1 cup baby spinach
- 1 cup buttermilk
- 1 teaspoon lemon juice
- ½ cup crushed ice
- 1 pinch salt

Directions:

Combine all the ingredients in a blender and pulse until smooth and well blended.

Pour the drink in glasses and serve it as fresh as possible.

Nutritional information per serving

Calories: 65

Fat: 1g

Protein: 3.9g

Carbohydrates: 9.2g

Edamame Almond Smoothie

Edamame is the green version of soy and just like dried soy, is healthy and loaded with fibers. It has a mild and fresh taste that complements well with the rich almonds. This drink is great for your digestive and immune system, but with an additional ingredient, such as pear or apple, it could also give you a much needed energy boost.

Servings: 4

Ingredients:

- ½ cup edamame beans
- 4 kale leaves
- ¼ cup blanched almonds
- 2 cups almond milk
- ½ ripe banana
- 4 ice cubes

Directions:

Mix all the ingredients in your blender and process until smooth.

Pour the drink in glasses of your choice and serve it as fresh as possible as it tends to lose nutrients in time.

Nutritional information per serving

Calories: 380

Fat: 32.6g

Protein: 8.3g

Carbohydrates: 20g

Sweet Potato Smoothie

Raw sweet potato is rich and creamy, sweet and delicious and has a high nutritional content, its main nutrients being beta-carotene. This recipe asks for a touch of spinach for a nutritional boost, but you can replace the spinach with any other fruit or vegetable.

Servings: 4

Ingredients:

- 1 ripe banana
- 2 cups fresh spinach
- 1 large sweet potato, peeled and diced
- 1 cup almond milk
- ½ cup crushed ice

Directions:

Combine all the ingredients in a blender and pulse until smooth and creamy.

Pour the smoothie in glasses and serve it as fresh as possible.

Nutritional information per serving

Calories: 213

Fat: 15.8g

Protein: 2.8g

Carbohydrates: 17.8g

Broccoli and Carrot Smoothie

Both broccoli and carrots are amazing veggies, healthy, loaded with nutrients and benefic for your digestive and immune system. Combine them and you get one of the healthiest smoothies ever. But also one of the tastiest if you add a touch of spices!

Servings: 4

Ingredients:

- 1 cup broccoli florets
- 2 large carrots, juiced
- 1 ½ cups almond milk
- 2 tablespoons blanched almonds
- ¼ teaspoon cinnamon powder
- 1 pinch nutmeg
- 2 tablespoons maple syrup

Directions:

Combine all the ingredients in your blender and pulse until smooth.

Pour the smoothie in glasses of your choice and serve it as fresh as possible.

Nutritional information per serving

Calories: 271

Fat: 23/1g

Protein: 3.6g

Carbohydrates: 16.8g

Spinach and Citrus Smoothie

This recipe is very basic and easy, but it has a lot of potential. You can use it as a base for your day to day drinks. Just add different fruits or vegetables and you're set to have a new drink every single time. Berries, Swiss chard, lettuce, cucumber, mint or even aromatic herbs are just a few of your choices.

Servings: 4

Ingredients:

- 2 cups spinach
- 2 oranges, cut into segments
- 1 cup plain yogurt
- 2 tablespoons honey
- 1 teaspoon orange zest
- 4 ice cubes

Directions:

Mix all the ingredients in your blender and pulse until smooth.

Pour the drink in glasses of your choice and serve it fresh and chilled.

Nutritional information per serving

Calories: 123

Fat: 1g

Protein: 4.7g

Carbohydrates: 24.4g

Spiced Pumpkin Smoothie

Pumpkin is not to be neglected! This colorful vegetable is high in beta-carotene and fibers and that makes it perfect for fighting against anemia or even heart-disease. A glass of this smoothie once in a while is a great addition to your diet.

Servings: 4

Ingredients:

- 1 cup pumpkin cubes
- 2 ripe pears, peeled and cored
- 1 cup fresh orange juice
- 1 cup plain yogurt
- ½ teaspoon grated ginger
- 2 tablespoons maple syrup
- Ice cubes for serving

Directions:

Combine all the ingredients in a blender and pulse until smooth.

Pour the drink in glasses and serve it with ice cubes if you want.

Nutritional information per serving

Calories: 166

Fat: 1.1g

Protein: 4.6g

Carbohydrates: 35.7g

Almond Avocado Smoothie

This rich smoothie is a delicacy for your taste buds. Both avocado and almonds are mild, but combined they create a well-balanced smoothie to brighten up your day. Just a touch of spinach is added for an extra nutritional kick.

Servings: 4

Ingredients:

- 1 ripe avocado, peeled
- 2 tablespoons blanched almonds
- 1 cup baby spinach
- 1 cup almond milk
- ½ cup water
- 2 tablespoons honey

Directions:

Combine all the ingredients in your blender and process at least 30 seconds until smooth.

Pour the drink in glasses of your choice and serve it fresh and chilled.

Nutritional information per serving

Calories: 291

Fat: 25.8g

Protein: 3.2g

Carbohydrates: 17.2g

Kale and Grapefruit Smoothie

This smoothie is amazing for weight loss because it has alow caloric content. Plus, the grapefruit is known for its benefits on boosting digestion and weight loss.

Servings: 4

Ingredients:

- 2 grapefruits, cut into segments
- 4 kale leaves, stems removed
- ½ cucumber, peeled and sliced
- 1 cup low fat yogurt

Directions:

Mix all the ingredients in a blender and pulse until smooth.

Pour the smoothie in glasses and serve it fresh and chilled.

Nutritional information per serving

Calories: 133

Fat: 1g

Protein: 6.1g

Carbohydrates: 17.9g

Pomelo and Spinach Smoothie

Pomelo is similar to grapefruit in terms of taste, but it has a higher nutritional content. Combined with spinach, it yields a fresh, slightly bitter smoothie, amazing for weight loss. Replace spinach with kale and you get a whole new drink or add another fruit and get a smoothie that tastes like dessert.

Servings: 4

Ingredients:

- ½ pomelo, peeled
- 2 cups fresh spinach
- 1 teaspoon chia seeds
- 1 cup almond milk
- 2 tablespoons honey

Directions:

Combine all the ingredients in a blender and pulse until smooth and creamy.

Pour the drink in glasses of your choice and serve it as fresh as possible.

Nutritional information per serving

Calories: 173

Fat: 14.3g

Protein: 1.9g

Carbohydrates: 12.5g

Aromatic Herb and Carrot Smoothie

This smoothie is amazing for a quick energy boost in the afternoon. The drink is a bomb of vitamin C and has benefic effects on your digestive system, providing your system with enough nutrients to keep going through the day.

Servings: 4

Ingredients:

- 2 green apples, peeled and cored
- 1 cup fresh parsley, stems removed
- 2 carrots, juiced
- ½ cup plain yogurt
- 1 cup almond milk
- 2 tablespoons maple syrup
- 1 pinch cinnamon powder

Directions:

Combine all the ingredients in your blender and pulse until smooth.

Pour the drink in glasses of your choice and serve it as fresh as possible.

Nutritional information per serving

Calories: 251

Fat: 14.8g

Protein: 3.8g

Carbohydrates: 28.7g

Gazpacho Smoothie

Gazpacho is a cold Mediterranean soup, but you don't need a bowl and a spoon to enjoy it, not when you have this delicious smoothie that tastes the same and has the same health benefits. Plus, it's versatile recipe so feel free to add any other vegetables you like to improve its taste and nutritional profile.

Servings: 4

Ingredients:

- 3 ripe tomatoes, peeled and seeded
- 1 cucumber, peeled
- ¼ cup fresh parsley
- ¼ cup fresh cilantro
- ½ cup spinach
- ½ celery stalk
- 1 tablespoon chives
- 1 cup plain yogurt
- 4 ice cubes

Directions:

Combine all the ingredients in a blender and pulse until smooth and creamy.

Pour the smoothie in glasses and decorate with a celery leaf just before serving.

Nutritional information per serving

Calories: 75

Fat: 1.1g

Protein: 5g

Carbohydrates: 11.2g

Spinach and Banana Smoothie

This rich and filling smoothie is great in the morning, but it can also be an energy booster in the afternoon. The spinach and banana come together perfectly and the walnuts make the drink smoother and richer. However, the walnuts have an intense taste so feel free to replace them with almonds or cashews.

Servings: 4

Ingredients:

- 1 ripe banana
- ½ cup walnuts
- 1 cup spinach
- 1 cup almond milk

- ½ cup plain yogurt
- ½ cup crushed ice
- 1 tablespoon honey
- 1 pinch cinnamon powder

Directions:

Mix all the ingredients in a blender and process until smooth and creamy.

Pour the drink in glasses and serve it fresh and chilled.

Nutritional information per serving

Calories: 300

Fat: 23g

Protein: 7.4g

Carbohydrates: 18.3g

Chocolate Spinach Smoothie

Chocolate can only be great, don't you think?! It sure does and spinach makes the drink so much healthier. Chocolate has its share of nutrients though: antioxidants, calcium, phosphorus, potassium and vitamin K are just a few of the nutrients found in chocolate.

Servings: 4

Ingredients:

- 2 cups fresh spinach
- ½ ripe banana
- 2 tablespoons raw cocoa powder
- 2 tablespoons honey
- 1 cup almond milk
- 1 tablespoon chia seeds
- 1 pinch cinnamon powder

Directions:

Mix all the ingredients in a blender and pulse until smooth and well blended.

Pour the smoothie in glasses and serve it as fresh as possible.

Nutritional information per serving

Calories: 232

Fat: 17.1g

Protein: 4g

Carbohydrates: 20g

Oatmeal Kale Smoothie

Are you on a rush to work in the morning?! No problem, you can now enjoy a quick breakfast on the run with this smoothie. However, don't make this a habit. Breakfast is breakfast and you shouldn't skip it every day.

Servings: 4

Ingredients:

- ¼ cup rolled oats
- 2 cups almond milk
- 6 kale leaves
- 4 ice cubes
- ½ ripe banana
- 1 tablespoon cocoa powder

Directions:

Mix all the ingredients in your blender. Pulse until smooth then pour the drink in glasses and serve it chilled and fresh.

Nutritional information per serving

Calories: 336

Fat: 29g

Protein: 5.1g

Carbohydrates: 16.5g

Peanut Butter Green Smoothie

Peanut butter is a classic, but apart from the usual sandwich, you can also use it for a delicious drink. A healthy one if I may add! This smoothie is thick, rich and filling, but also loaded with nutrients, like calcium, potassium and plenty of antioxidants. It's a real addition to your diet and even kids might tolerate it.

Servings: 4

Ingredients:

- ¼ cup peanut butter
- 1 cup fresh spinach
- 2 kale leaves
- 2 tablespoons chia seeds
- ½ cup plain yogurt
- 1 cup almond milk
- 2 tablespoons maple syrup
- 1 pinch nutmeg
- 1 pinch cinnamon powder

Directions:

Mix all the ingredients in a blender and pulse until well blended and smooth.

Pour the drink in glasses and serve it fresh and chilled.

Nutritional information per serving

Calories: 377

Protein: 11.5g

Fat: 25.6g

Carbohydrates: 24.4g

Hemp Seeds Green Smoothie

Just like chia seeds and flax seeds, hemp seeds are a bomb of nutrients, especially fibers, but also good fats. They make an excellent addition to any smoothie, not just this one.

Servings: 4

Ingredients:

- 1 ripe banana
- 2 Swiss chard leaves
- 1 cup vanilla yogurt
- 1 cup almond milk
- 1 tablespoon honey

Directions:

Combine all the ingredients in a blender and pulse until smooth and blended.

Pour the smoothie in glasses of your choice and serve it as fresh as possible as it tends to lose color and nutrients in time.

Nutritional information per serving

Calories: 229

Protein: 5.6g

Fat: 15.1g

Carbohydrates: 19.6g

Very Berry Spinach Smoothie

Spinach and loads of berries is what makes this smoothie such a delight for your taste buds! A touch of honey and vanilla complements the drink perfectly, but feel free to customize it. You can try adding a few spices or even replace the berries with other fruits. Cherries are a great alternative.

Servings: 4

Ingredients:

- 1 cup mixed berries
- 2 cups fresh spinach
- ½ ripe avocado, peeled
- 2 tablespoons honey
- ½ teaspoon vanilla extract
- 1 cup almond milk

Directions:

Combine all the ingredients in a blender and pulse until smooth.

Pour the smoothie in glasses and serve it as fresh as possible.

Nutritional information per serving

Calories: 245

Fat: 19.3g

Protein: 2.4g

Carbohydrates: 18.9g

Frozen Mango and Kale Smoothie

This chilled smoothie is amazing not only as drink, but also as dessert. Add more mango and you will get a thicker consistency that can be served with a teaspoon. As unusual as it sounds, this combination is delicious!

Servings: 4

Ingredients:

- 1 ripe mango, peeled, cubed and frozen
- ½ cup plain yogurt
- 1 cup almond milk
- ½ cup crushed ice
- ½ teaspoon vanilla extract

Directions:

Combine all the ingredients in a blender and process until smooth.

Pour the smoothie in glasses and serve it as fresh as possible.

Nutritional information per serving

Calories: 218

Fat: 16.3g

Protein: 3.6g

Carbohydrates: 15.7g

Tropical Green Smoothie

This drink brings together some amazing fruits and a few green leafy veggies and it actually makes them taste great. But what's even more important than taste is the high nutritional profile of this smoothie. Fibers, antioxidants, vitamin A and vitamin C are just a few of the nutrients found in this smoothie, but they are essential for a healthy lifestyle.

Servings: 4

Ingredients:

- 1 papaya, peeled and cubed
- 2 pineapple slices
- 2 tablespoons coconut flakes
- 1 cup coconut milk
- 1 ripe banana
- 1 cup buttermilk
- ½ teaspoon vanilla extract
- 1 cup fresh spinach

Directions:

Mix all the ingredients in a blender and pulse until well blended and smooth.

Pour the smoothie in glasses and serve it fresh and chilled.

Nutritional information per serving

Calories: 255

Fat: 15.9g

Protein: 4.6g

Carbohydrates: 27.6g

Chocolate Fudge Smoothie

This smoothie is a great way of introducing ingredients that you don't normally enjoy into your diet. And I'm talking about healthy ingredients like spinach or kale. Not everyone likes those, but you can hide their taste and color into smoothies like this one.

Servings: 4

Ingredients:

- ¼ cup coconut cream
- ¼ cup dark chocolate
- 1 tablespoon raw cocoa powder
- ½ cup crushed ice
- 1 cup coconut milk
- 1 cup water
- 2 tablespoons honey
- 1 cup fresh spinach

Directions:

Melt the coconut cream and dark chocolate together either on a double boiler or in the microwave.

Pour the mixture into a blender and add the remaining ingredients. Pulse until smooth.

Pour the drink in glasses and serve it fresh and chilled.

Nutritional information per serving

Calories: 285

Fat: 22.7g

Protein: 3.2g

Carbohydrates: 21.4g

Fig and Chard Smoothie

Now this is an exciting flavor combination. The ripe figs are sweet and delicate and for that reason you only need a bit of chard to balance it up and boost the nutritional content. However, if you're not familiar or don't like the chard, you can replace it with spinach, kale or collard greens.

Servings: 4

Ingredients:

- 6 ripe figs
- 2 chard leaves, stems removed
- 2 tablespoons maple syrup
- 2 cups almond milk
- ½ teaspoon grated ginger
- 1 tablespoon flax seeds

Directions:

Mix all the ingredients in a blender and pulse until smooth and well blended.

Pour the drink in glasses and serve it as fresh as possible.

Nutritional information per serving

Calories: 388

Fat: 29.5g

Protein: 4.5g

Carbohydrates: 33.1g

Lemonade Green Smoothie

Tangy and refreshing, this smoothie is amazing for summer. It truly is what you need on a hot summer day to cool you off, but also boost your energy level. The great thing about this recipe is that you can add more than one green leafy vegetable. In fact, just use what you have in the house as the final result will be tasty and healthy anyway.

Servings: 4

Ingredients:

- 1 cup fresh spinach
- 8 kale leaves, stems removed
- 1 cup plain yogurt
- ½ cup crushed ice
- ¼ cup lemon juice
- 3 tablespoons honey
- 2 mint leaves

Directions:

Combine all the ingredients in a blender and process until well blended and smooth.

Pour the smoothie in glasses and serve it as fresh as possible.

Nutritional information per serving

Calories: 133

Fat: 2.4g

Protein: 5.1g

Carbohydrates: 23.8g

Kale and Papaya Smoothie

This simple recipe is based on the healthy content of both papaya and kale. The trick for a smooth drink is to remove the stems from the kale. However, the kale is not compulsory and can be replaced with your favorite green leafy vegetable. Spinach is a great idea, but you can mix them up and be adventurous by adding some aromatic herbs too if you like their taste.

Servings: 4

Ingredients:

- 1 ripe mango, peeled and cubed
- 1 cup shredded kale
- 1 cup water
- 1 cup plain yogurt

Directions:

Mix all the ingredients in a blender and pulse until smooth and well blended.

Pour the drink in glasses of your choice and serve it as fresh as possible.

Nutritional information per serving

Calories: 88

Fat: 1g

Protein: 4.2g

Carbohydrates: 14.9g

Grape and Kiwi Smoothie

This smoothie is amazing for an energy boost in the afternoon. The grapes have plenty of natural sugar to give you energy, but the spinach and kiwi have a high nutritional content, including fibers and antioxidants. Overall, it's a delicious, healthy and rehydrating drink.

Servings: 4

Ingredients:

- 1 cup seedless green grapes
- 2 kiwis, peeled
- 1 cup fresh spinach
- 1 cup water
- ½ cup plain yogurt
- Juice from 1 orange

Directions:

Combine all the ingredients in a blender and pulse until smooth.

Pour the drink in glasses and serve it fresh.

Nutritional information per serving

Calories: 85

Fat: 0.6g

Protein: 2.5g

Carbohydrates: 17.7g

Dandelion Celery Smoothie

If you find young dandelion leaves at the market, definitely buy them! They are available especially in the spring, but a few days with this smoothie in your diet will detox your system and improve your general health.

Servings: 4

Ingredients:

- ½ bunch dandelion greens
- 1 celery stalk
- 2 green apples, peeled and cored
- 1 teaspoon grated ginger
- 1 cup plain yogurt
- 1 tablespoon honey
- ¼ cup crushed ice

Directions:

Mix all the ingredients in your blender and process until smooth.

Pour the drink in glasses and serve it as fresh as possible.

Nutritional information per serving

Calories: 109

Fat: 1g

Protein: 3.6g

Carbohydrates: 25.7g

Mediterranean Savory Smoothie

The great thing about smoothies is that they don't necessarily have to be sweet. Savory smoothies, like this one, are delicious and just as healthy. A touch of Mediterranean herbs brings this drink to live.

Servings: 4

Ingredients:

- 2 cups fresh spinach
- 1 celery stalk
- ¼ cup fresh cilantro
- 1 teaspoon fresh thyme
- ¼ jalapeno pepper
- 1 lime, juiced
- 1 cups water
- ½ cup plain yogurt

Directions:

Combine all the ingredients and pulse until well blended.

Pour the drink in glasses and serve it as fresh as possible.

Nutritional information per serving

Calories: 54

Fat: 0.8g

Protein: 4.4g

Carbohydrates: 6.1g

Cucumber and Parsley Smoothie

This smoothie has an intense flavor, but it's great for digestion. Moreover, it has a high water content so it will rehydrate your body and restock it on minerals and plenty of vitamins.

Servings: 4

Ingredients:

- 1 cup fresh parsley
- 1 large cucumber, peeled
- 1 red apple, cored and peeled
- 1 cup water
- ½ cup plain yogurt
- 1 tablespoon chia seeds

Directions:

Mix all the ingredients in a blender and pulse until smooth.

Pour the drink in glasses and serve it as fresh as possible.

Nutritional information per serving

Calories: 101

Fat: 3g

Protein: 4.2g

Carbohydrates: 14.8g

Thai Green Smoothie

This smoothie is rather savory, but tasty nonetheless and incredibly healthy. The cucumber, lime juice, turmeric and ginger make an excellent team to provide you with the much needed nutrients for a healthy life.

Servings: 4

Ingredients:

- 2 cucumber, peeled
- ½ avocado, peeled
- 1 lime, juiced
- 1 cup fresh spinach

- 1 teaspoon grated ginger
- ½ teaspoon turmeric powder
- 1 cup water

Directions:

Combine all the ingredients in a blender and pulse until smooth and well blended.

Pour the drink in glasses of your choice and serve it as fresh as possible.

Nutritional information per serving

Calories: 84

Fat: 5.3g

Protein: 1.7g

Carbohydrates: 10.2g

Cucumber and Dill Smoothie

Cucumber and dill is a classic combination in the Mediterranean cuisine. It tastes great and it's refreshing and rehydrating. The recipe also calls for avocado and lime juice to make the smoothie richer, but also brighten it up slightly. It's a well-balanced and healthy drink, perfect for your morning meals.

Servings: 4

Ingredients:

- 1 large cucumber
- ½ celery stalk
- 2 kale leaves
- 1 ripe avocado
- ¼ cup fresh dill
- 1 cup buttermilk
- ½ cup crushed ice

Directions:

Mix all the ingredients in a blender. Pulse until smooth and creamy then pour the smoothie in glasses and serve it as fresh as possible.

Nutritional information per serving

Calories: 163

Fat: 10.6g

Protein: 5g

Carbohydrates: 15.2g

Mango Bliss Smoothie

This rich and fragrant smoothie is thick and tastes just like dessert. It will surely satisfy your sweet cravings and spare you the need of eating sugar in its processed form. This smoothie contains natural sugar and loads of nutrients so it's healthy and a much better choice than any other dessert.

Servings: 4

Ingredients:

- 1 ripe mango, peeled and cubed
- 4 chard leaves
- 1 pear, peeled and cored
- 1 ripe banana
- 1 kiwi, peeled
- 1 cup almond milk

Directions:

Mix all the ingredients in a blender and process at least 30 seconds until well mixed.

Pour the smoothie in glasses and serve it as fresh as possible.

Nutritional information per serving

Calories: 242

Fat: 14.7g

Protein: 3.1g

Carbohydrates: 28.8g

Parsley and Pineapple Smoothie

Sounds unusual, doesn't it?! But it's so delicious! You have to try it and see for yourself before judging this recipe. The parsley is enough to flavor it, but it's not overpowering the other ingredients. What you get is a smoothie that has great benefits on digestion, both pineapple and parsley being known for boosting the digestive system.

Servings: 4

Ingredients:

- ½ cup fresh parsley
- 4 kale leaves
- 2 thick slices pineapple
- 1 ripe pear, cored and peeled
- 1 cup water
- ½ cup plain yogurt
- 1 tablespoon honey
- 4 ice cubes

Directions:

Combine all the ingredients in a blender and process until smooth.

Pour the smoothie in glasses and serve it as fresh as possible.

Nutritional information per serving

Calories: 110

Fat: 1g

Protein: 3.1g

Carbohydrates: 24.9g

Persimmon and Spinach Smoothie

This thick and fragrant smoothie is a delicacy. The ingredient list is short, but this recipe relies on the high nutritional profile of the persimmon and spinach and that's all it needs.

Servings: 4

Ingredients:

- 4 persimmons, peeled and seeded
- 2 cups baby spinach
- 1 cup ice cubes
- 1 cup coconut water

Directions:

Combine all the ingredients in a blender. Process at least 30 seconds or until the smoothie is well blended.

Pour the drink in glasses and serve it as fresh as possible.

Nutritional information per serving

Calories: 79

Fat: 0.2g

Protein: 1g

Carbohydrates: 11.1g

Pear and Aloe Vera Smoothie

If you have stomach and digestion problems, this drink is a life saver. The pear boosts the digestion process, but the aloe sooths the stomach. They both have a high content of fibers and vitamins, but are also quite mild in terms of taste so the final drink is well balanced.

Servings: 4

Ingredients:

- 2 ripe pears, peeled and cored
- 1 leaf aloe vera
- 4 kale leaves
- 1 ripe banana
- 1 cup water

Directions:

Combine all the ingredients in a blender and pulse until well blended and smooth.

Pour the drink in glasses and serve it fresh and chilled.

<u>Nutritional information per serving</u>

Calories: 123

Fat: 0.1g

Protein: 2.7g

Carbohydrates: 30.9g

Apple and Lettuce Smoothie

Simple and easy, this smoothie uses cheap ingredients, but the final result is nutritious and delicious, refreshing and rehydrating, great for spring or summer when there is plenty of apples and young lettuce.

Servings: 4

Ingredients:

- 2 green apples, peeled and cored
- 6 romaine lettuce leaves
- 1 ripe banana
- 1 tablespoon lemon juice
- 1 cup plain yogurt
- ½ cup crushed ice
- 2 tablespoons maple syrup
- 1 pinch cinnamon

Directions:

Mix all the ingredients in a blender and process until well blended and smooth.

Pour the drink in glasses and serve it as fresh as possible as it tends to lose color and nutrients in time.

Nutritional information per serving

Calories: 145

Fat: 1g

Protein: 3.9g

Carbohydrates: 30.7g

Watermelon and Lime Green Smoothie

The heat of summer requires you to drink plenty of liquids and this smoothie does just that – restores the water in your body, but also brings vitamins and antioxidants. It's a refreshing and simple drink and it doesn't need anything else.

Servings: 4

Ingredients:

- 1 cup seedless watermelon cubes
- 2 cups fresh spinach
- 1 lime, juiced and zested
- 1 cup crushed ice
- ½ cup coconut water
- 1 tablespoon chia seeds

Directions:

Combine all the ingredients in a blender and pulse until smooth.

Pour the drink in glasses and serve it as fresh as possible.

Nutritional information per serving

Calories: 69

Fat: 2.5g

Protein: 2.4g

Carbohydrates: 8.4g

Summer Green Smoothie

Summer is an explosion of fruits and veggies so why not take advantage of that?! This smoothie takes a few summer staple fruits and combines them into a nutritious and filling smoothie that does a great job at restoring your energy level when you most need it.

Servings: 4

Ingredients:

- 4 apricots, pitted
- 2 ripe peaches, pitted
- 4 kale leaves
- 1 cup almond milk
- ½ cup plain yogurt
- 4 ice cubes

Directions:

Mix all the ingredients in a blender and pulse until smooth.

Pour the drink in glasses and serve it fresh and chilled.

Nutritional information per serving

Calories: 229

Fat: 14.9g

Protein: 6.1g

Carbohydrates: 21g

Blueberry and Lettuce Smoothie

This smoothie combines a family favorite – blueberries – with lettuce which tends to be slightly bitter, but highly nutritious. However, in this recipe, the bitter taste is mellowed down by the blueberries and pears so the final drink is enjoyable and so healthy.

Servings: 4

Ingredients:

- 4 lettuce leaves
- 1 cup fresh or frozen blueberries
- 2 ripe pears, peeled and cored
- 1 cup water
- ½ cup almond milk

Directions:

Mix all the ingredients in your blender and process until well blended and smooth.
Pour the drink in glasses and serve it fresh.

Nutritional information per serving
Calories: 151
Fat: 7.4g
Protein: 1.4g
Carbohydrates: 23.2g

Coconut Green Smoothie

The coconut milk is so delicate. It's only fair to pair it with just as delicate ingredients just to keep the balance right. Kale, peaches and a touch of mango seems like the best combination, although you are free to add any other ingredient you want to create a whole new coconut based drink.

Servings: 4

Ingredients:

- 1 cup coconut milk
- 4 kale leaves, stems removed
- 2 ripe peaches, pitted
- ½ ripe mango, peeled
- ½ cup crushed ice

Directions:

Mix all the ingredients in a blender and pulse until smooth.

Pour the drink in glasses and serve it fresh and chilled.

Nutritional information per serving

Calories: 190

Fat: 14.4g

Protein: 3.8g

Carbohydrates: 15g

Cilantro Limeade Smoothie

Cilantro is fairly fragrant, but the lime balances it perfectly, creating a refreshing and delicious smoothie. The nutritional profile is loaded with vitamin C and other powerful antioxidants, making this drink benefic for boosting the immune system.

Servings: 4

Ingredients:

- 2 cups fresh spinach
- ½ cup cilantro
- 1 ripe banana
- 1 lime, juiced and zested

- 1 teaspoon grated ginger
- 1 cup water
- 6 ice cubes

Directions:

Mix all the ingredients in a blender and pulse until well blended.

Pour the drink in glasses and serve it fresh and chilled.

Nutritional information per serving

Calories: 57

Fat: 0.1g

Protein: 0.8g

Carbohydrates: 9.4g

More great books by Jonathan Vine

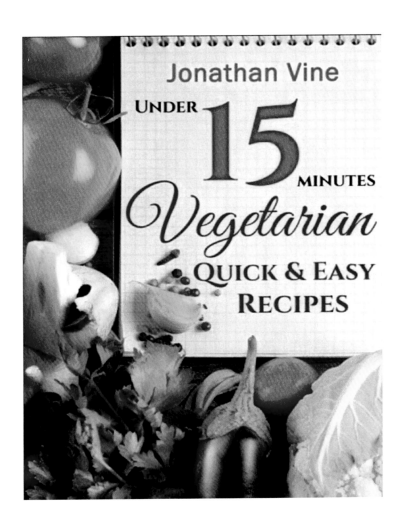

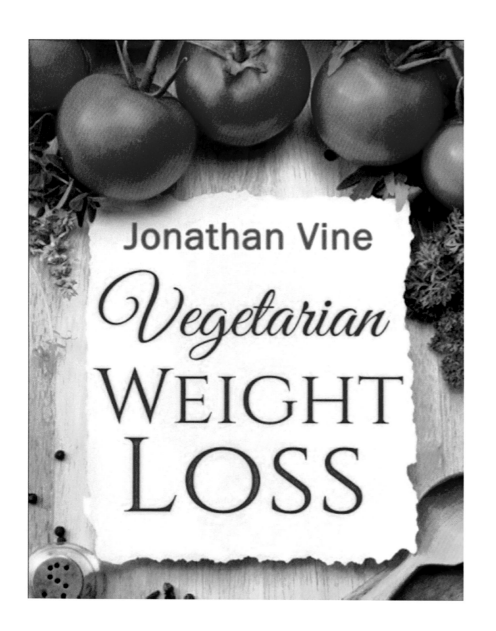

Made in the USA
Middletown, DE
18 February 2015